Get Your Hopes Up

Nichole Schreiber
Quintin C. Lindblad

Get Your Hopes Up

30 Days of Shifting Your Perspective

Published by Erie First Assembly

Published by Erie First Assembly of God.
Available on Amazon.com

ISBN: 1983592315
ISBN-13: 978-1983592317

Dedication

We would like to dedicate this book to our church family at Erie First Assembly. Thank you for letting us serve you every week and more than anything, thank you for trusting us to share the greatest hope of all time! It is through you that we will love like Christ loves, build what Christ desires to build and ultimately send His hope into this world.

Acknowledgements

First and foremost, we would like to thank our families for cheering us on as we have tackled this project. Thank you for giving us the space to write late into the night, edit during family breakfasts and present this book as the end result. You are our biggest fans and our greatest inspirations.

Second, we want to say a huge thank you to the staff at Erie First Assembly. Your support and patience as we have grinded out this project have been a great blessing. We could not have done it without you believing in us.

Third, we owe the biggest thanks to Jonathan McCray and Anna Dambacher for their design work on the book cover and the sermon art that went with this project. You both are amazing and we appreciate your artistic excellence. Let's do it again next year!

Contents

Introduction

Part 1: Breaking Chains

Part 2: Fighting For Hope

Part 3: Loving Others Well

Part 4: Loving Christ Above All Else

Conclusion: Taking This into Your Everyday Life

Introduction

Have you ever believed for something great or close to impossible only to be told, "Don't get your hopes up?" It happens more often than it should, but that doesn't make it good advice. We have called this devotional book *Get Your Hopes Up* because we believe that when you surrender your personal view of things over to Christ and allow Him to shift your perspective, you will find the most hopeful and exciting way of life is waiting to be experienced.

This is certainly not to say that life will become sunshine and rainbows, free from circumstances or trials. Anyone writing that type of book probably doesn't truly respect you or the very real life that you live. We know that life comes at everyone with cheap shots, sucker punches and pain unimaginable at times.

But we also know Jesus! And that changes everything. Jesus is the surest, safest, most rewarding bet you could ever make with your life. And we believe that when you understand that, your hopes will soar through the roof!

Before we dive into this journey together, allow us to briefly introduce ourselves and give you some background so you know who you are hearing from as you read. Also, be sure to use the "Notes" section at the end of the book for your reflections.

Nichole Schreiber, Author of Parts 1 & 2

Nichole Schreiber is the Lead Pastor of Erie First Assembly. After spending 10 years working with Chi Alpha Campus Ministries alongside her husband Joel, God moved Nichole in an exciting new direction that led to her being confirmed as Erie First's Lead Pastor in February of 2017. Both Joel and Nichole are ordained with credentials from the Assemblies of God.

Joel and Nichole have three rambunctious, hilarious, lovely girls: Cecily, Haley and Mercy. Joel loves to be outdoors and Nichole reads and writes in her spare time. They are out to spend their whole lives for Jesus in every way possible.

Quintin C. Lindblad, Author of Parts 3 & 4

After spending almost 10 years in the sales and business world, God redirected Quint's path quite abruptly. He had spent a significant amount of time away from music when an opportunity to help a local church came into his life, leading him to a calling that he never saw coming. What started out as a volunteer role eventually led to Quint becoming a full-time pastor. In November of 2017, he was hired as the Worship & Family Pastor at Erie First Assembly. His heart is to help people take the Word of God and practically apply it into their everyday, ordinary life.

He and his wife Erin have 4 awesome children who are astonishingly close in age: Anderson Charles – age 3; Preston Oakes – age 1; Charlotte JoAnn – also age 1; and Bennett Cooper – newborn.

Part One:

Breaking Chains

Written by Nichole Schreiber

Dead Spots 1

The angel said to the women, "Do not be afraid, for I know that you are looking for Jesus, who was crucified. He is not here; he has risen, just as he said. Come and see the place where he lay."
- Matthew 28:5-6

Each time we celebrate Easter, we are taking time to recognize that what was dead is now alive. In Matthew 28 we read, *"…at dawn on the first day of the week…there was a great earthquake."* The angel of the Lord was coming down out of heaven and rolling the stone away from the door of the tomb. The crucified and resurrected Christ proved to be alive. He had defeated death, hell, sin and the grave! It is far too much to sum up in a single paragraph.

What in your life feels dead?

We can feel dead emotionally at times. There are seasons of life when we have weathered storms that are so heavy we just turn our emotions off so we feel nothing at all. Somehow that feels safer to us.

An internal emotional struggle can also make you feel dead inside. Perhaps you are stressed out or overwhelmed. Maybe you are struggling with depression and anxiety to the point that it is hard to get up in the morning. You might be facing an impossible situation and just can't see a way out. When the thoughts come to your mind, they feel like they could drown you. Or maybe your insecurities are so deep; they have completely stopped you from pursuing any of your dreams because you are afraid to fail again. You simply cannot face another rejection.

Perhaps you are working through a relational dead spot. You could be wrestling through conflicts with a friend. You could be spending your days picking up the pieces of your life after a divorce. Or the death of a friend or family member may have left a gaping hole in your heart. I believe sometimes the pain and hurt from a broken heart is worse than physical pain.

Lastly, you may be feeling dead spiritually. At some point in your life you were very close to God, but somehow you drifted. Somehow a separation happened and now God feels very far away. Church may have become just a routine and you feel like you're simply going through the motions; checking the box and hoping it counts.

Whatever might feel dead in your life, you can be sure that Jesus overcomes it all. He is the only one who can breathe life on what is dying in your life. The world doesn't have the keys. Another new relationship doesn't have the keys. A winning lottery ticket won't fix what is broken. But Jesus brings life to whatever is dead or dying in and around us!

Romans 8:11 says, *"The Spirit of God, who raised Jesus from the dead, lives in you. And just as God raised Christ Jesus from the dead, he will give life to your mortal bodies by this same Spirit living within you."* The same spirit that God used to raise Jesus to life on Easter is the same Spirit that dwells within you today. Get your Hopes Up!

1) Do you have a dead spot emotionally, relationally, or spiritually in your life?

2) How can the hope of Easter change the reality of that struggle?

*The Spirit of God, who raised Jesus from the dead, lives in you.
And just as God raised Christ Jesus from the dead, he will give
life to your mortal bodies by this same Spirit living within you.*
- Romans 8:11

When I was in college, my roommates and I loved to play practical jokes on each other. One day I came home and discovered the power was out. I lit candles, read by flashlight and ate peanut butter and jelly because I couldn't cook with our electric stove. I sat around for hours in the dark. Then I went into my bedroom and, out of habit, turned on the light switch. I noticed the fan starting to move. I reached up and turned one of the light bulbs and it turned on! My roommates had unscrewed every single light bulb and unplugged everything from the socket. I sat around for hours thinking the power was out. Little did I know it wasn't a power problem. The connection was broken.

Romans 8:11 describes the power that raised Christ from the dead as the same power that has been made available to us through the Holy Spirit. The question we have to wrestle with is this: are we connected to it? If not, it is not a power problem; it is a connection problem. Are we tapping into the power of the Holy Spirit?

*Stand firm then, with the belt of truth buckled around your waist,
with the breastplate of righteousness in place, and with your feet
fitted with the readiness that comes from the gospel of peace. In
addition to all this, take up the shield of faith, with which you can*

extinguish all the flaming arrows of the evil one. Take the helmet of salvation and the sword of the Spirit, which is the word of God.
- Ephesians 6:14-17

As we are living our everyday lives, we need to be connected and protected by the Spirit of God. If we put on the full armor of God – the belt, the breastplate, the boots, the shield, and the helmet – we are covered on all sides. No matter if the attack comes from the sky, the ground, the side or the front – we are covered.

When we put on the armor of God we are really putting on Christ. Romans chapter 13 references the armor of light and then says, *"Rather, clothe yourselves with the Lord Jesus Christ, and do not think about how to gratify the desires of the flesh."* The Apostle Paul is saying: "Don't live on the enemy's level. You don't belong there. You are not on his level. You are above him and you can live in victory. The road is straight and clear of roadblocks to get to Jesus!"

Insert your name as you read these statements:
In *(your name)* there is defeat, but in Christ there is victory.
In *(your name)* there is condemnation, but in Christ there is salvation.
In *(your name)* we receive a sin nature, but in Christ we receive a new nature.

1) How can you get more connected to God today?

2) Which part of the armor of God from Ephesians 6 do you need most right now?

Therefore, if anyone is in Christ, the new creation has come: The old has gone, the new is here! **- 2 Corinthians 5:17**

God is determined to overcome our brokenness. Our walk with Jesus is about transformation. We will not always be as we are now. Things will change; things must change. The desire for transformation lies deep within every human heart. This is why people enter therapy, join health clubs, get into recovery groups, read self-help books, or try new diets. The possibility of transformation is the essence of hope.

Psychologists say the single most toxic belief to a relationship is the idea that the other person cannot change. We have a tendency to think of our faith in Jesus as "only avoiding the bad things." We begin cutting out the things in our life that we shouldn't do. We stop cussing, or quit looking at pornography, or stop gossiping about others. But that's only half of it.

There is a positive movement in the Gospel bringing about the new creation and ushering us into the resurrection life. We find this message again and again throughout scripture. Ephesians 4:22-24 says, *"You were taught with regard to your former way of life, to put off your old self, which is being corrupted by it's deceitful desires; to be made new in the attitude of your minds; and to put on the new self, created to be like God in true righteousness and holiness."*

New life is a matter of both taking off the old self and putting on the new. Following Jesus isn't just about what we say "no" to, but it is also about what we say "yes" to!

So if you have been lying: stop! And start speaking truth. If you have been stealing: stop! And start giving to people. If you have been distracted and not following God closely: stop! Turn and chase Him with all that you have!

You can change. Things will change. You can get out of bad relationships. You can stop bad habits. You can change directions. You can become more like Jesus. You don't have to live this way forever.

A friend once told me a story about a really hard time he was experiencing. He met up with a friend for coffee and for 90 straight minutes, this friend just looked him in the eye and said, "You don't have to live this way" over and over and over until he believed it. This is the message of the gospel. You don't have to live the old way. You can change.

1) What can you start saying YES to that will build your spiritual life?

2) What do you need to change about your character, and what positive movement can you make to move into that new way of living?

*Forgetting what is behind and straining toward
what is ahead, I press on toward the goal to win the prize for
which God has called me heavenward in Christ Jesus.*
- Philippians 3:13-14

Our spiritual enemy, Satan, is constantly trying to bring to mind the failures of our past. He accuses, lies and discourages. His greatest desire is that we would quit striving, give up and live in our mess. When we are feeling defeated about our past decisions, we can remind our spiritual enemy of Easter Sunday. On that day, he was defeated once and for all!

Christ is calling us to press on and forget the past, to forget what is behind and strain towards what is ahead. In Greek, the term "forgetting the past" is defined, "to treat with thoughtless inattention, to willfully neglect, to leave behind intentionally, to cease remembering."

For some, Satan has been haunting us with our past. And while we cannot change our past, Christ can change our future. The truth is God can deal with the messy situations we create. He works best with messy lives. When we repent and turn from our sin, Christ forgives us. In that forgiveness, even with really bad past decisions, we can ask ourselves this question:

*"Who shall separate us from the love of Christ? Shall
trouble or hardship or persecution or famine or nakedness or
danger or sword?"* -**Romans 8:35**

Paul, the author of Romans, enthusiastically answers his own question in verse 37: *"No, in all these things we are more than conquerors. Not in our own power but through Christ who loved us."*

It is not in our own strength; it is not in our own power, but it is through the power of the risen Christ. If we are believers in Jesus Christ and His resurrection power, we are more than conquerors; we are more than overcomers. In fact, the little Greek word that is translated as conqueror, or victor, is the word *"inikao"* which means, "to win or be victorious." But that is not the word that is used in this passage. The word used here is *ihupernikao. iHuper* means "exceedingly more than." This verse is declaring, "we are way more than winners, we are *ihupernikao*!"

What took a lifetime to tear us down, God can heal and vanquish in a second. Sometimes negative thoughts plague us and contribute to bringing our hopes down. But through Christ we are victors and overcomers!

Here is something practical from the Word that we can do when those negative thoughts start to come in: *"…demolish arguments and every pretension that sets itself up against the knowledge of God. We take captive every thought. We make it obedient to Christ."* **- 2 Corinthians 10:5**

Because of what Jesus did on the cross and how He rose again three days later, you are an overcomer. Your past can't hold you down. Get your Hopes Up!

1) What in your past do you need to forget so you can reach for what is ahead?

Down But Not Out   5

Repent, then, and turn to God, so that your sins may be wiped out, that times of refreshing may come from the Lord. **- Acts 3:19**

Samson was a man in the Old Testament; we can find his story in Judges 16. His fatal flaw was that he was an emotionally driven person, not a Spirit-led person. That can be a problem for a lot of us. Our emotions get out of control and we end up letting those feelings drive us rather than letting the Spirit be our guide. Samson's downfall didn't all happen all at once, though. It was a series of small, bad decisions. He was supposed to be delivering God's people, but instead was a shackled prisoner whose eyes had been gouged out. His past had caught up with him. His past was personified in the big wooden grinder that he was carrying around in circles.

Some of us are living in this moment that we find Samson in. We've done things we can't undo, we're embarrassed, we're ashamed, we've hurt people we love, and we've strayed from what God created us to do. We have ended up walking around in circles, carrying our regrets with us.

But just when it looks like Samson failed way too much for God to love him, much less use him, we see a God who still accomplishes His purposes through a man that repeatedly could not get it right. You see, just because you are down, doesn't mean you are out. And even if you have failed at something, that doesn't make you a failure. Failure is an event, but it is never a person.

So Samson stands in the temple, a giant coliseum with huge pillars that support the weight of the entire structure. Samson cries out to God in repentance, *"O God, please strengthen me. Strengthen me just once more!"* He is broken and finally repentant. It is no longer about him; it is now all about God. He realizes that the main character in the story isn't him; it is God. Even after our failures, God can still accomplish His purposes.

Judges 16:29-30 records, *"Then Samson reached toward the two central pillars on which the temple stood. Bracing himself against them, his right hand on the one and his left hand on the other. Then Samson said, "Let me die with the Philistines!" Then he pushed with all his might, and down came the temple on the rulers and all the people in it. Thus he killed many more when he died than while he lived."*

He pushed the pillars with all of his might. Everything came crumbling down and he destroyed more of God's enemies as he died than in all the years that he lived. He was a hero. He did what God asked him to do; he sacrificed his own life and ultimately obeyed God. Repentance is a game changer. God can restore His purposes for your life when you repent and turn from your sins.

1) What failures do you feel have disqualified you from God using you?

2) What can you repent of today so God can restore His purpose in your life?

Blind Spots 6

Though a righteous man falls seven times, he rises again.
- Proverbs 24:16

I cannot speak for you, but I am a repeat offender. Despite my best efforts, I often find myself stuck in the same patterns of sin. I have been a pastor long enough to know that I am not alone in this though. It is something everyone deals with.

The danger with sin if we are not careful, is that our hearts can become hard to it. By letting unholy things dwell in our minds, our hearts lose their sensitivity. When we decide that coarse joking is no big thing or that sexual immorality is ok because it is culturally acceptable, we lose sensitivity. When we decide that profanity is just part of what we have to do in the workplace to fit in, our hearts begin to grow calloused. When we ignore the conviction of the Holy Spirit, we develop a calloused heart.

Allow me to ask you a question that will be the litmus test for the softness of your heart: Do your inconsistencies bother you? If your reaction is, "What inconsistencies?" then you might have a problem.

If you admit you have some inconsistencies but they don't bother you then take great warning in love as you read this, because your heart may be hard and you don't even realize it. Through repentance, God can show you what part of your heart is hard; He will ask you to change attitudes, actions, and thought patterns that you have held on to for a very long time; maybe even things that you didn't realize were displeasing to

Him. He will reveal your blind spots. And we all have them. Personally, I would rather lay awake at night frustrated with my sin, not getting it right but working on it, than ignore and justify it, refusing to change.

People typically respond to failure in one of two ways: remorse or repentance. Remorse projects the failure internally. It tears us up and we convince ourselves we are terrible or have no future. Sometimes we live as victims and blame everything around us on circumstances as a result. Remorse focuses on the bad, looking back at all the things that were done wrong.

However, repentance owns the failure. Repentance sounds like "I'm sorry. I made a mistake. I own it." "Re" means to turn. We turn from our lower sinful ways to God's higher, holy ways. We change directions. We shift our perspective.

You can't undo the bad deal that you did, but you can repent. You can't unsay what you said, but you can repent. You can't un-look at what you looked at, but you can repent. You can't go back in time and change what happened, but you can repent and ask God to redeem the failure! That should certainly get your hopes up!

1) Do your inconsistencies bother you?

2) How do you usually respond to failure - with remorse or repentance?

Be kind and compassionate to one another, forgiving each other, just as in Christ God forgave you. **- Ephesians 4:32**

One key ingredient to forgetting what is behind us is living out the commandment of forgiveness. God commands us to forgive others, just as we have been forgiven. Basically, the Scripture says if we don't forgive others our faith won't work. Everything that comes from God comes through faith *(Ephesians 2)*. So we are in big trouble without faith!

If we want mercy, we have to give mercy. If we want forgiveness and grace we have to give forgiveness and grace freely. I am glad God doesn't put a limit on how many times He forgives me. I am glad the rule is 70 times 7. Have you done the same wrong thing at least 70 times 7 and God has still forgiven you for it?

Forgiveness is NOT forgetting.

Confusion sometimes arises because Scripture says that God *"will remember our sins no more."* *(Hebrews 8:12)* However, God knows everything and cannot "forget" as if He had no memory of our sin. But still, His promise in Psalm 103:10 is that He will never use our past against us. When we come to Jesus, He is not thinking about the sin of our past. Jesus is never withholding because of our shortcomings. He is not slow to bless us because of our past sins.

In the same way, when we forgive those in our life, we are committing to not hold their past against them. When we bring up the past and use it against others, we are showing that we have not truly forgiven them. If the first thing that comes to mind, when we see that person is the sin they committed against us, we have not forgiven them entirely.

Forgiveness is NOT a feeling.

We also cannot wait to forgive until we feel like forgiving. We may never get there. After we have obeyed God's command to forgive, our emotions begin to heal. Feelings follow choices. When we do what we know is right in the Word of God, our feelings will catch up.

Feelings have an important role in forgiveness. In order to fully forgive someone, we must let God bring to the surface the emotions or pain that we feel. Burying or ignoring those feelings can cause long-term effects on our spiritual life. God's gentle healing process can begin after we have admitted what was hurt and why it hurt.

Find a trusted friend, a group leader, a family member or a pastor and be honest about the pain you are encountering. Journal your thoughts and feelings. Forgiveness will lead to freedom!

1) Make a list of people that come to mind that you need to forgive. Pray this simple prayer: Lord, I forgive (name) for (what they did to hurt you) even though it made me feel (share your feelings).

Part Two

Fighting For Hope

Written by Nichole Schreiber

The Next Small Step

*In this world you will have trouble! But take heart
I have overcome the world!* **- John 16:33**

In the book of Genesis, we find the account of a man named Abram. Well, his given name was Abram. He was later renamed Abraham. But called by either name, we see him wrestling on multiple occasions with doubt. He struggles with doubt that weighs him down; doubt that causes him to make bad decisions; doubt that creates problems; and doubt that ultimately suffocates his hope.

In this world, Abram had trouble. In Genesis 12, there is a famine and he decides to go to Egypt for a season to escape the difficult conditions. He prompts his wife, Sarai, to tell the officials that she is his sister in an attempt to secure their safety and well-being.

Abram comes up against a situation that is hard to see the end result so he takes things into his own hands. Can you relate? He doubts that God will provide. He doubts that God can make a way for his family to survive the famine. And as a result, Abram compromises his integrity and he lies.

Then again in Genesis 16, we read that God had made a promise that Sarai would bear a son. They waited and waited, but no baby. Abram begins to doubt that God will make good on his promise. He starts to justify and calculate. After all, he is getting old. After a while, he begins to think that God forgot the promise altogether. Regardless of the specific thoughts that went through his head, he was confused. Abram again doubts

God's provision. He doubts God can or will give him a son. So again, he takes matters into his own hands and sleeps with his Egyptian slave, Hagar, who becomes pregnant with Ishmael.

Doubt had disillusioned Abram's hope. That can happen in our lives, too. Maybe you haven't had a job for several months and the doubt that God will provide you with one begins to weigh you down. Or maybe you aren't married yet; instead you are the person in everyone else's wedding. Doubt that God remembers your desires can begin to make your heart heavy. When we come up against a situation where we can't see the end result, we can sometimes insert doubt instead of hope just like Abram did.

The truth is that there is no such thing as trusting God without unanswered questions. If we knew all the answers, there would be no need to trust Him. He purposely doesn't tell us all the details because He wants us to trust Him. He purposely doesn't always make the provision known because He wants us to place our hope in Him. I believe God only shows us the next small step in the dark parts of our lives because in the dark we stay very close to the person who is holding the flashlight.

1) What doubts are you having that are stealing from your hope?

2) What is the next small step God is asking you to take?

> *Do not be afraid, Abram. I am your shield,*
> *your very great reward.* **- Genesis 15:1**

How do you respond when you're discouraged? Do you ever lay in your bed at 2 o'clock in the afternoon and pull the covers over your head? Do you ever sit at your kitchen table blankly staring, wishing you were any place but there?

In Genesis 15, God shows up and reminds Abram of the promise He had made. He says in verse 1, *"Do not be afraid, Abram. I am your shield, your very great reward."*

Now that's a pretty encouraging word from the Creator of the universe, who says I, personally, am your shield and your great reward. But here is how Abram responds in Genesis 15:2, *"...Abram said: Sovereign Lord, what can you give me since I remain childless and the one who will inherit my estate is Eliezer of Damascus?"*

In essence, Abram takes God's great word of encouragement and says something like: "Blah blah blah. You still haven't given me the only thing I wanted. How is this time going to be different?" Then he goes back to life as he knows it. Abram is discouraged. He has lost all hope. He is weighed down.

Discouragement dries us up. That is what discouragement does. The things we used to find fun or refreshing become dull and boring. They stop exciting us. We may read a good book or listen to our favorite song and feel nothing. David describes discouragement in Psalm 63 in this way: *"You, God, are my God, earnestly I seek you; I thirst for you, my whole being longs for you, in a dry and parched land where there is no water."*

The enemy will try to discourage you because he knows you must have courage to overcome the attacks that he launches against your hope. So by eliminating your courage, he can tear down your hope. But it is important to know that courage doesn't look just one certain way. Courage does not always roar with boldness. Sometimes courage is the quiet voice at the end of the day saying, "I will try again tomorrow."

I believe depths of faith can vary. One depth delivers us from trials, but another depth takes us through them. It doesn't take nearly as much faith to pray and get delivered from something as it does to continue to walk in hope that God is going to show up.

When God's power seems like it isn't being manifested, when we feel like we are wasting our days, when our heart is not healing from grief or pain the way we thought it would – but we still hold onto hope anyways – that is a whole new level of faith. It is in the face of discouragement that we grow in faith. Don't avoid those trials, lean in and go through them with courage!

1) When was the last time you felt discouraged?

2) When was the last time you showed courage in dealing with a trial?

My times are in your hands; deliver me from the hands of my enemies, from those who pursue me. **- Psalm 31:15**

What happens to hope when the promise isn't here yet? What happens when we thought for sure that we heard from God, but then nothing manifests? When we thought we knew God's character, we trusted in Him, but it appears He isn't showing up like we expected Him to? What happens to our hope when we experience this type of delay?

In Genesis 15, God and Abram have a talk and God makes a promise. He essentially says, "I'm going to give you a son. That son is going to give you offspring as many as the stars in the sky. Look up, look up at them!"

In Genesis 16, a little over a decade has passed and Abram is still waiting for the promise. I don't know about you, but I can't wait two minutes in the drive through without getting a little edgy. And yet here he is, with no sign of what God told him almost a full decade later. Understandably, he's feeling older and crankier. The delay has done a number on his hope.

Then, in Genesis 17, Abram is ninety-nine years old. God shows up and changes his name to Abraham. Abraham means "father of multitudes, father of many." I can imagine Abraham, in the delay, feeling a little awkward about this name change since he is father of zero sons to Sarah. It would be like God changing my name to Taylor Swift. I can't do even one of her dance moves.

God then changes his wife's name to Sarah and gives them the name of the son who is going to be born to them, Isaac. It's almost like a movie teaser because Sarah still does not get pregnant for another full year. Can you imagine? The delay is still threatening the hope of God's promise.

Has God made you a promise that you're still waiting for? Did you feel like God said, "If you keep praying for him, I will help him beat that addiction." or "if you stay faithful to me, I will provide for your family." Or maybe it was "If you take a risk, I will give you more than you would ever dream." When God speaks, and we don't see, it is very hard to hold onto hope. When weeks, months, or even years pass by, hope can fade.

In Genesis 21:1-2 we read this, "*Now the Lord was gracious to Sarah as he had said, and the Lord did for Sarah what he had promised. Sarah became pregnant and bore a son to Abraham in his old age, at the very time God had promised him.*" We shouldn't be surprised that God came through. It's what He does. God keeps His promises. You can hope again because God keeps His promises!

Galatians 6:9 speaks to the apparent delay of some of God's promises. *"Don't be weary in doing well because in due time we will reap if we faint not."* Due time means: the time God thinks is right. God is the author of time, and we can trust Him to fulfill His promises. We can hope even when there is delay.

1) What promise has God made to you that you are still waiting to see happen?

*Therefore we do not lose heart. Though outwardly
we are wasting away, yet inwardly we are being
renewed day by day.* **- 2 Corinthians 4:16**

God fulfilled Abraham's long awaited, long
loved promise of providing him a son named Isaac. So
it's quite amazing that we find this twist in the story in
Genesis 22: *"Then God said, 'Take your son, your only son,
whom you love—Isaac—and go to the region of Moriah. Sacrifice
him there as a burnt offering on a mountain I will show you.'"*

You may be familiar with the story of Abraham
and Isaac. By God's command Abraham builds an
altar, arranges the wood, binds up his son (the boy he
waited decades for), reaches out his hand, takes the
knife and begins the motion to sacrifice his son – but
then God stops him. Abraham looks up and there is a
ram in the bushes that he will use instead for the
sacrifice.

Genesis 22:14 then says, *"So Abraham called that
place The Lord Will Provide…"* In Hebrew, "the Lord will
Provide" is spoken "Jehovah Jireh."

I have always used the name "Jehovah Jireh" in
the context of someone needing a physical object. I
would pray that Jehovah Jireh would provide for
financial needs or vehicles for missionaries or grocery
money for families. But when I read this passage again,
I see God, Jehovah Jireh, not just providing the physical
object of the ram that Abraham needed. I believe
Jehovah Jireh, the Lord our Provider, showed up with
hope that day. He provided the hope that Abraham

needed in the darkest, most confusing moment of his life. Jehovah Jireh, The Lord Provides. It is possible that Abraham meant this about more than just the ram, but also about hope.

In Romans 4, Paul gives the synopsis of Abraham's life and says this: *"Against all hope, Abraham in hope believed and so became the father of many nations, just as it had been said to him, 'So shall your offspring be.' Without weakening in his faith, he faced the fact that his body was as good as dead—since he was about a hundred years old—and that Sarah's womb was also dead. Yet he did not waver through unbelief regarding the promise of God, but was strengthened in his faith and gave glory to God, being fully persuaded that God had power to do what he had promised. This is why 'it was credited to him as righteousness.'"* The words "it was credited to him" were written not for him alone, but also for us. God will credit us with righteousness – if we believe in him who raised Jesus our Lord from the dead. He was delivered over to death for our sins and was raised to life for our justification!

In this passage from Genesis, Abraham gave glory to God. The Hebrew word for Glory is *Kabod*, which literally means "weight or heaviness." When we are losing hope, we are giving too much weight to the doubt, delay and discouragement. When we give all the glory, or weight, to God, He will provide us with all the hope we need!

1) Can you think of a situation where God provided you hope when you needed it most?

2) What sticks out to you most in the passage listed above from Romans 4?

Renewed Hope

12

When Jesus saw him lying there and learned that he had been in this condition for a long time, he asked him, "Do you want to get well?" **- John 5:6**

In this verse from John 5, Jesus is talking to a man who had waited for 38 years by the pool of Bethesda to be healed. The story tells us that when an angel of the Lord would stir up the pool, whoever got into the water first would be healed. This man watched year after year as others received healing. They left with breakthrough, as he sat, helpless, by the pool. I can imagine year five probably started feeling difficult. Can you even dream what year 35 felt like?

When Jesus approached this man, he asked him a fairly basic question: *"Do you want to get well?"* It seems like an odd question to ask a man who has committed so many years to sitting by the pool for a chance of healing. But Jesus always sees our hearts. Jesus knew this man had lost hope. He had retreated to the idea that he would never experience this miracle. And so Jesus asks to stir up this man's hope.

Where in your life have you given up hope? Maybe you were hopeful God would provide a certain job for you, but it hasn't happened yet so you have decided to settle into the one you have. Perhaps you have been hoping for a breakthrough with your spouse or your children, but nothing seems to be changing. As believers in the risen Christ, we have to think differently when we don't see the instant results we want to see. God is always working. If we are praying about it, God is working on it! Romans 12:12 says, *"Be joyful in hope, patient in affliction, faithful in prayer."*

Our hearts can get hard toward God, even resentful, when we feel like we have hoped for something for a long time but God hasn't provided it. When we get into that position, our hearts often go blind to hope. Sin makes it difficult for us to see God's goodness. We may begin to question God's character or wonder if He is holding out on us. This creates a chasm between God and us.

To prevent this, we have to continually repent and ask God to forgive us for not trusting Him fully. He has our best in mind, and we cannot question His timing or His care for each of our lives. In the meantime, when we say we have "hope" for a change, we are proclaiming that we have confident anticipation. After all this time waiting, Jesus asked the man by the pool and He asks us today: *"Do you want to get well?"*

As Christians, we know that no matter how many peaks and valleys we go through in life, this whole thing is heading toward a huge and forever celebration. Where the world sees only a hopeless end, believers in Christ see an endless hope! This hope doesn't just exist in heaven but it is available for us – right here, right now!

1) In the waiting, has your heart turned hard in some area of your life, and you have given up hope?

2) Who in your life reminds you to have hope in Christ?

We are therefore Christ's ambassadors, as though God were making his appeal through us. We implore you on Christ's behalf: Be reconciled to God. **- 2 Corinthians 5:20**

In Mark 2 we find a story of Jesus teaching in Capernaum, probably at Simon Peter's house, and there are massive crowds all around Him. Four friends are carrying a paralytic man on a mat hoping to see him healed of his affliction, but there is literally no way to approach Christ with this crippled man in tow. It is too hard a task. The circumstances seem impossible. Then these friends come up with a creative solution: the roof! They lower him down and Jesus, seeing their faith, says *"your sins are forgiven."* He then heals him of all his physical ailments too! The man gets up, walks and everybody praises God.

Now these are some good friends. They carried this paralytic man; they shimmied onto the roof for him; they truly loved him. If it weren't for them, he would be absolutely hopeless. Have you ever felt that hopeless? Where you just wish someone, somewhere would help you out of the situation that you are in.

The reason the gospel is called the Good News is that it provides mankind with hope. Hope for our paralyzed moments. As Christians, we are no better than anyone else. We have just discovered the Good News and we have experienced God's love and forgiveness. He has given us the privilege of helping others experience it, too. We don't have to convince people of the truth and hope of the gospel; that is God's job. Our job is to genuinely love the people in our lives and to share the experiences of our life with them. One of those life experiences is our faith. It should be a natural part of our relationships to share our faith with those around us.

If you struggle with sharing your faith in Christ because of fear, the solution for that is found in 1 John 4:18, "...*perfect love drives out fear*." God is perfect love. Ask God to increase your love for people to such a level that you care more about their eternal destiny than your own personal comfort. This will begin changing the way you think about people.

For a solid year of my life I prayed this prayer: "God, help me to have a deep love for people and a deep conviction of sin." He began to show me how He viewed people. Seeing people in their lost state moved Jesus to distress, even tears. When we criticize and judge people for making bad choices or for not understanding the ways of God, we are not being like Him. When we can see people the way God sees them, we can fight for them. The friends in Capernaum went to great lengths to help their friend come face to face with hope. Let's strive to be those types of friends for those around us.

1) How did you first encounter the hope of Jesus? Take time to thank God for those that helped you come face to face with Jesus!

2) How do you believe Jesus views those who don't yet know Him personally?

Since you are precious and honored in my sight, and because I love you, I will give people in exchange for you, nations in exchange for your life. **- Isaiah 43:4**

As a believer, your assignment is to go deeper with Jesus and take as many people with you to eternity as you possibly can. To take the hope of Jesus Christ to your neighborhood, your city and your world. This verse from Isaiah 43 explains that if you will give your life to take His hope to others, God will give people to you to love. He will entrust you with people that He wants you to love into the kingdom of God.

The Lord Jesus viewed the winning of one soul as worth more than the whole world. He spent much of His time talking with one person at a time about His relationship to God.

There are 3 dominant metaphors describing our relationship to Christ in the Scriptures: sheep to a shepherd, child to a father, and bride to a bridegroom. All of these suggest a real, true, meaningful relationship. Sheep are guided, loved, taken care of and saved from peril by their shepherd. Children are their father's most valuable possession. They love, discipline and provide for them always. Brides are completely devoted, committed and selflessly giving to their bridegroom. Jesus wants us to tell the people in our lives about the hope of a meaningful relationship with Him. He wants us to help others grow in hope. Christ wants us to unselfishly share the hope that we have found in Him.

It doesn't have to be hard or complicated or flashy. Sharing the hope of Jesus just needs to be intentional. It will take sacrifice, commitment and uncomfortable conversations at times. Christ publicly called for people to come to faith in Him on many occasions: *"I am the bread of life; he who comes to Me shall not hunger, and he who believes in Me shall never thirst" (John 6:35); "I am the light of the world; he who follows Me shall not walk in the darkness, but shall have the light of life" (John 8:12)*

Jesus did not only proclaim this publicly. He also invited people to accept him personally with close and intimate relationships. Jesus brought Philip, Matthew, Peter and Andrew to faith with the call, *"Follow Me." (Matthew 4)* In John 4, He met a woman at a well and brought her to salvation. In Luke 19, He found Zaccheus the tax collector, whom He led to a confession of sin, repentance, and faith. In John 3, He taught Nicodemus about the new birth. In Mark 10, He led blind Bartimaeus to believe in Him.

We need to continue explaining to people both publicly and personally who Christ is and the hope that He offers. Someone out there did it for us, and now it's our turn. This is actually the chief command that Christ gave us in the Great Commission, *"…go and make disciples." (Matthew 28:19)* The risk of not telling our friends, family, and even strangers is the risk of their eternal separation from God; their shepherd, father, and bridegroom.

1) Make a list of names God has brought to mind who you can share the message of Hope with.

Part Three

Loving Others Well

Written by Quintin C. Lindblad

The greatest among you will be your servant. For those who exalt themselves will be humbled, and those who humble themselves will be exalted. **- Matthew 23:11-12**

So many Scriptures point to this principle of living graciously, it is hard to know where to start on such a big subject. How do you pick just one verse or even one passage when there are so many? How do you condense the topic to a page or two and think you've done it justice? I ultimately landed in Matthew 23 because Jesus not only tells us how to love others well in these two verses but He also demonstrated to us with His life in the way only God's perfect Son could. This is the foundation of loving others and doing it well – being a servant to all.

I have often said that the charge we find in both James 4 and 1 Peter 5 to *"Humble yourselves before the Lord and He will lift you up"* is first and foremost a warning. It's not simply a pathway to promotion where we let God do the lifting up. It is a strong warning to humble ourselves so that we do not find ourselves getting humbled by life or circumstances. He desires that we live humbly, not seeking personal gain but trusting in His plan for our lives.

When we interact with those around us, it can be very easy to compartmentalize people into boxes or categories that are comfortable to us. We assess where someone lives, the car they drive, or the career choices they have made and we tend to make assumptions based on what we see. Most of the time, it isn't from a place of disdain or even judgment; it is just our second nature. We feel like it helps us to process who someone is based purely on what we can see with our eyes. A blunt way to describe this habit would be *lazy*. It is honestly just lazy to box people up this way and not truly get to know them. We are shortcutting the process of relationship based simply on what we see.

But another way to describe this behavior – an honest and sobering way – would be the opposite of living graciously. "To live from a position of grace" is to assume the best in any and every one. It is to strive to see each person as their Father in heaven sees them. When we see decisions being made that we disagree with – that the Bible disagrees with – and we want to make a snap judgment, we need to remember that the Bible also calls the people we are judging *"Christ's lost sheep"* (Luke 15) that He came to find and redeem. We need to look at them with compassionate eyes. We need to desire their rescue and redemption.

When we do this, we will automatically forfeit any position of personal gain because we will humbly be working towards the gracious reception of a lost soul. This is what it means to be a servant to all. What an awesome opportunity to help the Kingdom grow. It's amazing we have such a part to play!

1) Do you feel you live from a position of grace towards others?

2) Do you justify times when you choose to not live graciously based on circumstances?

For whoever wants to save their life will lose it, but whoever loses their life for me and for the gospel will save it. **- Mark 8:35**

How different would our lives look if we lived from a position of grace over personal gain? If we actually sought to know someone before deciding who they may or may not be? What if we began to live by the mantra of "taking the low seat?" Maybe you have never heard this expression, but several years ago I listened to a message from Morgan Snyder of Ransomed Heart Ministries that changed the way I approach, well, everything!

He explained in this message that "to take the low seat" is to enter every conversation, conflict, interaction and circumstance with the pre-determined outlook that we have no rights or entitlements. It is to put our faith above our feelings; it is to love our fellow man more than we love ourselves. As Jesus says in today's verse from Mark 8, we must surrender our lives to truly save them.

When we are determined to live 100% for Christ, life is no longer about the strength of our will but the total surrender of it. It is our human nature to cling to what we believe to be right; to be true; to be most important. But through the power of Christ inside us, we can make the choice to abandon our personal agenda and see situations as He does. When we find ourselves in varying situations that challenge us, we can seek His help to step outside of ourselves and view things how He views them.

How does He see the family member who is bringing us a trial for what seems like the 1,000th time? Or the friends that think only of themselves? Or the boss that doesn't respect us and takes credit for work that we have done? Do you really want to know how God sees these people? He sees them as His own and His heart is for their redemption!

When we get ahold of this, everything begins to change. 1 Timothy 2:4 tells us that God *"wants all people to be saved and to come to a knowledge of the truth."* His heart is for their salvation and as His redeemed, we have a part to play in that. We can step into a supernatural way of living when we let go of our way and latch onto His way. This is counterintuitive; it denies how we are born in the natural. This way of life is only possible with the Holy Spirit working through us. How sweet it is to live so intimately with Christ that we can play this role!

The most practical, basic way to start living a surrendered life is to regularly "take the low seat." Look for ways in your everyday life where you can serve others by seeing things from their perspective. And better yet, look for ways that you can see those same people from Father God's perspective! This will change absolutely everything. Hope will begin to flow out of you!

1) What are some ways – who are some people – you can begin to serve by taking the low seat?

2) Spend some time in prayer asking God to help you see others the way He sees them.

We have this hope as an anchor for the
soul, firm and secure… **- Hebrews 6:19**

This particular verse might be the most quoted verse on hope in all of Scripture. I've seen it on more than one coffee mug and I know at least a couple of people who have it hanging in their homes. And of course I would never belittle anyone hanging Scripture in their home to find inspiration, but this verse is so much more than something catchy to wear on a t-shirt. All Scripture is intended to help us grow and live as Christ has called us to live. So go ahead, hang all the artwork and buy all the coffee mugs - but let's get it inside of us too! Let's take the words to heart and meditate on what they are saying: there is a hope so firm and secure that when we get ahold of it, we will have a truly great hope to offer others!

Many years ago an old Marine taught me this valuable lesson: "You can't teach what you ain't is!" And that, my friends, is about as close to a Gospel truth as you can get without just preaching the Gospel. What he meant was you can't teach something you don't live out and you can't give something you don't first possess yourself. So here in Hebrews we are being told where we can find a hope that surpasses all other hopes. This hope is so strong that it not only reaches our soul, but also anchors it. This hope attaches itself, goes as deep as possible and becomes immovable. Wow!

When we are living from a grace-filled position and regularly taking the low seat in challenging circumstances, life can feel really hard. Life can feel unfair or even overwhelming. And frankly, if we are relying on our natural strength to do these two things, it will be overwhelming. It's not something we humans can do with our inner, natural strength. We need a source that is beyond us. We need a hope that anchors us. And we are promised here in Hebrews that such a hope exists.

When we cling to Christ as our hope, we can offer grace and humility to others, which ultimately will offer hope to others. It offers a hope that there is more to life than being selfish; a hope that there are people in this world that care about others; a hope that might be unexplainable with words but that they will feel in their hearts. This is called leading by example and offering hope to others with the greatest resource you have been given – your life!

So as you seek to live graciously and to see others as their Father in heaven sees them, remember where to find your hope. Remember where to place your hope. Place it firmly in Christ and let Him be your anchor. Let Him tether you to the Father and be your source so that you are not beat up by loving others, but you are empowered by it!

1) Where do you place your hope?

2) Are you attempting to love others from your own strength or with Christ as your source?

The Next Generation   **18**

*One generation commends your works to another;
they tell of your mighty acts.* **- Psalm 145:4**

As we make strides in our walk with Christ, our influence is meant to grow. The desire of our Father is that we would not just set our life on cruise control, but that we would increase in Kingdom impact with every passing week, month and year of our faith. One author I love says it something like this, "The Christian life is not a coast downhill. We aren't just waiting to catch a flight to heaven." As we have already discussed, we have role to play. And what could be better news?

One of the most humbling things about God the Father is that He doesn't stop the process at redeeming us; He also restores us and equips us to fight in the battle for His Kingdom. And a chief way we can do that is through our influence we have on those around us.

We have influence through our beliefs, words and actions. We have influence by how graciously we live and by how much we serve others. We can influence our spouse, our siblings, our co-workers and our peers. But I believe the greatest place we can have direct Kingdom influence is over our children. King David tells us in this 145th Psalm that we have the responsibility of *"proclaiming God's works to the next generation."* Our children deserve parents who faithfully reveal God's goodness and prepare them to do major damage for the Kingdom!

I just stumbled across a picture of my oldest son on stage with me right around his 3rd birthday. He loves music, but more specifically he loves *worship music.* He regularly skips the first half of his class at church so he can watch his daddy lead the church in worship. When he was about 2 years old, he started asking my wife when he would get to join me on stage. I decided to let him come up for our opening song right before his third birthday. Few people worshiped because they were so enamored by the spectacle of my "mini-me" on stage for the first time. It may seem inconsequential or even silly in the grand scheme of things. But when I posted the photos online and shared the experience with my friends or family who couldn't be there, I wrote, "Be a hero for your kids. That's a target you won't ever regret aiming for."

I believe one way we proclaim the goodness of God to the next generation is by walking side-by-side with them through experiences that show them firsthand, they worship the same God we do. They have access to the same God we are talking about and telling them about.

When we successfully instill this hope and faith into the next generation, we will live with a joy and hope for the future that is indescribable. Because honestly, how could we describe with mere words the hope we have as parents when we see our children worshiping and communing with God their Father?

1) In what ways are you proclaiming God's goodness to the next generation?

2) If you do not have children or yours are grown, are you finding other ways to pour into the next generation?

Your boasting is not good. Don't you know that a little yeast leavens the whole batch of dough? **- 1 Corinthians 5:6**

Before you close the book and decide that I have forgotten the point of this devotional as a tool for increased hope, read on a bit more. I am not changing the subject, but I also am not going to pretend that we can shift our perspective in a 30-day window without being challenged a bit (or a lot)! And all good challenges start with a question, so allow me to ask you one: have you considered the part you play in your church family - both good and bad? Have you considered that where you place your hope has an affect on all those around you? Let's unpack this.

The specific issue in 1 Corinthians 5 is one of sexual immorality. So it could be easy to say "Quint, come on. That's an easy one! Of course it's wrong and of course it would negatively affect the church." But I'm not going to let anyone off easy here. I would propose that while this blatant sin was absolutely an issue that needed dealt with, it was actually the cause of the sin that got the individuals – and the church – into trouble. And what was the cause? The cause was where these Christians had placed their hope.

So much of our sin comes from believing we will find hope, fulfillment, joy, etc. in places that were never meant to give us those things. And this can be as extreme as sexual immorality or as simple as finding our identity in what we do for others as opposed to who we are in Christ.

As pastors, we are constantly helping people get plugged in to various places in the church. We love it when people serve and quite frankly, the church needs people to serve! But the flip side to that coin is that we never want people to find their identity in what they do for the church. Whether it is worship ministry or kids ministry or welcoming new guests – those things are not who you are; they are simply a chance to serve others and worship God for what He has done in your life. But when taken to an extreme, finding your identity in what you do is actually a sin. It is worshiping the act of service and finding your hope there instead of worshiping God and finding His true hope that always fulfills.

So back to the effect on the church – when we are out of alignment, it absolutely throws off those around us. In 1 Corinthians 11, Paul warns the church against coming together with separate agendas or with hearts that are not right with Christ. When we do this, we can actually bring heartache on others. But when our hope is found in Christ alone, we can worship with others, serve others and bless our Father in heaven in the most rewarding way. Or should I say - in the most hopeful way?

1) In what places have you sought to find hope? Are you relying solely on Christ to fulfill you?

2) What repentance and change do you need to seek to offer hope to your church family?

Now faith is confidence in what we hope for and assurance about what we do not see. **- Hebrews 11:1**

Faith and hope. These are two amazing traits that are unique to human beings. I suppose dogs or cats and other animals may have hopes in the simplest possible form, but here we are speaking of true and deep hope with a cognitive understanding of how it is exercised in our lives. Whether an animal has faith or hope is a debate I don't care to win. But how we, as Christians, understand the role of faith and hope in our lives is beyond important. It changes everything.

Faith is believing in something you cannot see with your eyes and believing at such a level that you have full confidence in its existence or its eventual existence. Christians and non-Christians alike have varying faiths and hopes. Faith in their favorite sports team; faith in their employer to provide a paycheck; or faith in their political party.

The thing about faith is, it builds on itself by looking back at prior successes. Confidence grows when we can see evidence in our past of something or someone coming through. But hope is unique because hope looks forward. Hope is the substance of looking forward with faith strengthened by the past.

When we place our hopes in the promises of God that are found throughout His Word, we have so much to look forward to. We have an undeniable, unreachable height of hope that demands a gracious outlook on life. Hopes as great as the ones we get to call our own should change everything. They should change how we love our families; how we lead our children and how we interact with the un-churched all around us.

Would your co-workers or employees, your bosses or your friends, describe you as someone with a uniquely different (and hopeful) perspective on life? They should! We are equipped with hopes of a coming restoration in our future and also a renewed, saved life in our present. We can live daily in the promise from 1 John 4 that we *"..are from God and have overcome them, because the one who is in you is greater than the one who is in the world."* If this was the only promise we had been given, it would be more than enough. Yet we have been given countless more to place our hopes in.

So let us seek to live hope-filled lives that bless others. Let us look back on all the good things God has done in our lives and let those things be reminders – altars of praise – that we serve a God who is in the business of coming through.

Spend some time thinking through all that He has done in your life to this point. Think through the circumstances that led to this book ending up in your hands. Maybe it was parents who faithfully taught you the Word. Maybe it was a friend who invited you to church and introduced you to the most beautiful Savior, Jesus Christ. Maybe it was simply God being patient with you while you ran from Him until you came to your senses and realized you should have been running to Him. Whatever the case is, let your faith be built and let it fuel your hope for an even better future!

1) What events from your past can you look on to build up your faith and increase your hope?

Become the kind of container God can use to present any and every kind of gift to His guests for their blessing.
- 2 Timothy 2:21 (MSG)

This week we have tackled a lot. We have explored living from a position of grace, taking the low seat, thinking about the generation that is coming on behind us, and more. We have covered so many facets of loving others well and what that could specifically look like in the day-to-day of your life. But to wrap up this section, I want to talk generally. That might seem like a backwards way to approach a topic – specific first and general towards the end – but in this scenario I feel it works. Allow me to explain.

In this verse from 2 Timothy 2, Paul is painting with the broad brush of being useful for *"any and every kind of gift"* that the Father might want to shower upon someone. This is our target. We want to be useful for whatever God might need of us. Sometimes we get so bogged down by the specifics that we are useless in the day-to-day. Here we are being encouraged to be useful in all possible avenues that God might need us.

I've seen this happen in so many different areas; someone studies so hard for a specific thing that they are paralyzed by any other circumstance that comes their way. It's not the way it is meant to be. We need to be servants of all, willing to do all that might be required. To do this we must cling to the charge in Romans 13 to only owe the debt of love to those who are around us.

Paul follows up 2 Timothy 2:21 with the charge to *"Run away from infantile indulgence. Run after mature righteousness."* Being willing to do whatever task our Father asks of us is a sign of Spiritual maturity. That is the kind of maturity we are after. To walk through life with Christ as our guide and the power of the Holy Spirit working inside of us should absolutely result in a humility that says, "Here am I, Lord. Use me however You see fit!"

This is what living graciously and taking the low seat is all about. This is how it is lived out in the most practical way – being willing to do anything God asks of us! His requests are always meant for His glory and our good. The two go hand-in-hand. When we hang on to our way of doing things, we are clinging to immaturity and robbing God of the chance to grow us up. We are missing out on an internal hope that is indescribable and we certainly will not have such a hope to offer anyone else.

So take a minute as we close this week's topic of "Loving Others Well" and do some soul-searching. Ask yourself, and ask your Father where you have been placing your hope. Are you the kind of Christian that God can use for any and every kind of work? Are you spiritually mature enough to lay down your way and embrace His way? If not, take a step today! Pray to the Father that you would let go of your desired works and embrace the opportunities He puts in your path everyday. It's honestly as simple as that! When you take that step, you have walked towards a new place of spiritual maturity!

1) What has been your greatest lesson from this section on Loving Others Well?

Part Four

Loving Christ Above All Else

Written by Quintin C. Lindblad

Not Self-Help

On that day you will realize that I am in my Father,
and you are in me, and I am in you. **- John 14:20**

Without this fourth part of our 30-day journey together, a lot of what we have shared could easily get labeled as some type of Bible-inspired self-help – some positive Christian vibes and principles that could make your life a little more hopeful. But that's not what we are about; that's not what we have set out to do. We are about True Hope and we know exactly Who that hope comes from. It comes from Christ inside of us! Christ working inside you and me and invading our everyday life is the only way to sustain this life of hopefulness. The question is how do we get Him to the center?

I was once at an event where the author of The Shack, William Paul Young, was speaking. He said something that completely rocked me. He actually said several things that rocked me, but the specific thing from that night that changed the way I view myself and others was this: if you grabbed the Gospel with both hands and squeezed it with everything you had, this verse would be the final drop that came out. He shared that this verse from John 14 is the smallest, most finite link in the Gospel chain. He believes it to be the change agent for the entire world because it is revealing the power of Christ inside of us and the power of the Father working through Christ.

When we realize that Christ's work on this Earth was a total outflow of His relationship with the Father, we will know exactly where our source comes from. God the Father never intended for us to do this on our own. His desire for our lives is that we would live in such close relationship with Him that our actions would be a result of that intimacy; that our moves would be dictated by what our Savior would have us do in various situations. Life becomes a response – an act of worship – each and everyday. God's plan was never for us to digest a bunch of Scriptures and then try to apply their principles by our own strength or willpower. He wants to co-labor with us.

This is what we mean by "Christian Self-Help." Far too often people get caught up in an action-based Christianity that requires understanding the Word from an academic viewpoint and then trying like crazy to apply it in their daily actions all on their own efforts. But we are called to live by faith. This means we can live with the faith that the Holy Spirit inside of us is all that we need to be triumphant in various circumstances.

We don't have to totally understand, but we can still live in it. When we are abiding in Christ and finding our source to be our relationship with Him, this faith becomes real. This faith begins to show up in our daily life without any effort of our own. It is a faith in the One who has called us and who desires intimate relationship. This is why it's not self-help; it's Christ's help!

1) Would you describe your understanding of Christianity to be one of relationship or of actions based on lessons from the Bible?

2) Are you willing to live day-by-day in the overflow of relationship with Christ?

*I am the vine; you are the branches. If you abide
in me and I in you, you will bear much fruit;
apart from me you can do nothing.* **- John 15:5**

Living on mission. Living by faith. Living with purpose. Living like Jesus. These are all popular and common phrases that are used in churches everywhere. And they all have their place. They all mean great things and result in great work being done. But today I want to challenge you to the one phrase that gives life to all these others – living in Him. We are handed the promise of a lifetime when Jesus tells us *"If you abide in me and I in you, you will bear much fruit."* It is a promise that should stir up faith, action, purpose and so many other things because it is the absolute foundation of our hope-filled life.

Jesus spells things out so clearly here. It's like He is giving us the shortcut to a life of spiritual success. *"If you abide in me... you will bear much fruit."* We seriously have one job! He has called us to abide in Him as He abides in us and then there will be fruit. How amazingly simple! It is a classic "If this, then that" scenario. Our job is not to produce fruit in our lives. Our job is to abide in Him and entrust the fruit (and the pace of its growth) to the vinedresser. When we truly get this, we will begin to eliminate all pressure and performance from our lives. We will know that our job is much less about action and much more about relationship with our Savior!

In my first book, I told the story my wife and I

lived through in 2015 when we lost a baby to miscarriage. It was a gut-wrenching experience. Our first pregnancy had been so ideal and gone so well that we were not at all prepared for such an event. It wasn't even on our radar, and it all happened so fast but also seemed so slow at the same time. It is something that shook us greatly, and in the weeks and months that followed, we found ourselves learning all new levels of trust in each other and in Christ.

What we found to be the thing that got us through was abiding in one another. I define abiding as "placing your well-being and safety in the care of another." When we hand over our very existence to the One who gave it to us in the first place, He is able to come in and do more than we could ever attempt on our own. Ultimately, Erin and I did not just abide in each other. We were abiding in our Savior and He was giving me the strength to be there for her and giving her the strength to be there for me.

It is a hard thing to fully explain, but the reality is this: when we abide in Christ – when we place our well-being and safety in His hands – He comes through in the most amazing ways. Sometimes He does it through those He has placed in our lives, sometimes through our time with Him as we read the Bible, pray and worship. Usually it is a combination of the two!

When we trust and allow this to happen, we find a safety, calmness, and peace that is only possible through surrendering our care to Him. When we are truly abiding in Him, we will have the greatest hope!

1) Would you say that you have surrendered your well-being and care completely to Jesus?

...Father, the hour has come. Glorify your Son,
that your Son may glorify you. **-John 17:1**

At the close of John chapter 16, Jesus is telling His disciples of all that is to come. He is unpacking the relationship between Himself and His Father. He is warning of the abandonment He is about to face and also the triumph He will bring for the Kingdom of God. It is quite a passionate message that is delivered with little or no fluff – the time is coming and regardless of all else, He is ready.

As we turn to chapter 17 with this context in mind, we see our Savior asking His Father to *"display the bright splendor of His Son" (MSG)* because He knows that He is our representation of Father God. Jesus Christ's time on this Earth was our window to see who God the Father truly is. His ministry, mission and purpose were all meant to reveal the Father to us and then redeem us to salvation.

We serve a God who came down to our level, emptied himself of everything, and completed His mission with pinpoint accuracy. There were no missed steps or miscues. This is why He alone is worthy of all our praise. He paid the ultimate price to buy us back and reveal the true plan for our lives! The call to abide in Him is not one of duty or obligation; it is one of tremendous privilege. It is both humbling and awe-inspiring.

As I read through John 17 years ago, I wrote this in the margin of my Bible: "Jesus takes this chapter to remind and affirm the mission of His life with the Father. This is healthy, worshipful and soul restoring. It places Father God at the head and recharges Christ for the completed work of His life." This exercise of ascribing worth to God actually recharged Christ and helped Him to finish strong. He was worshiping through this prayer and He was being filled up through His worship. It is exactly how God intended it to be.

If ascribing worth to the One who deserves glory recharged Jesus Christ himself, then of course we will find the same recharge in our lives when we lift up our Savior for all that He has done. We have this amazing and beautiful example of what it means to worship God. We also find Christ reminding Himself of all that He did through His ministry. This is good and this is healthy.

As we discussed at the end of Part Three, our faith grows in strength when we look back and see the areas of breakthrough we have known. It gives us increased hope for all that is to come. And Christ himself participated in this exercise.

As you enter into prayer and worship, let your hope be fueled by these activities. Remind yourself of all that God has done in your life and all of the various times He has come through. Remind yourself of the obedience you have walked out. Let that be an encouragement to you! He's done it before and He will do it again. You've done it before and you can do it again!

1) What reminders can you give yourself of times that God has come through and areas that you have walked in obedience?

To be mature is to be basic. Christ!
- Colossians 1:28 (MSG)

I was not often described as a mature child or teenager. Actually, I was never described as mature. But when I stumbled upon this verse in Colossians, I felt like I could actually attain maturity for once. The Apostle Paul is telling us that our maturity is not based on how much we know or can spout off in a discussion. Our maturity is based on keeping the message simple and pure, communicating it well to all who will listen. The NIV translation says it this way: *"He is the one we proclaim... that we may present everyone fully mature in Christ."*

When we keep Christ at the center of our message – His life, death and resurrection – we are preaching the simple gospel of redemption and casting the widest net possible to all who will hear. We are living as mature Christians who understand the one job we were given was to *"Go and make disciples of all nations."* (Matthew 28:19) We are worshiping with our actions when we obey this great command.

Of course it is profitable for us to dive deeper into the ways of God. He is a well that is infinitely deep and we will never find the bottom. In fact, just a few pages before Colossians 1, you will find a verse in Ephesians chapter 3 telling you *"to grasp how wide and long and high and deep is the love of Christ..."* But even in this grasping for more, we land on His great love. We land on the basic and foundational love of Christ that spurs us on to share salvation with others. How amazing and how cohesive the Word of God is!

This is why loving Christ comes above all else. Loving Christ is the foundation of everything. We need to love Him with all that we have if we are ever going to love others in the most basic and fundamental way. If we are ever going to present salvation to them without agenda or human tendencies getting in the way, we are going to need to love Him with all that we have. We are going to need to be mature by staying "basic" with others. Lead them to Christ and then let the Holy Spirit and healthy Gospel Community take them deeper. But our job is the basic job of living in relationship with Christ and sharing His salvation in total love.

May we be a people who are seen as mature not because of our ability to debate spiritual things, but because of our fundamental approach to reaching those who are lost. Christ's desire is that we would worship Him through our obedience. Let's be obedient in this work and see people come to know their Savior! That is a way to show love to our Savior that will return awesome dividends!

1) Have you considered where your perception of maturity comes from and are you willing to surrender it back to Christ if it is anything other than being basic?

This is how we know that we love the children of God:
by loving God and carrying out his commands. **- 1 John 5:2**

Sometimes it can almost feel like too much. Christian radio, Christian apparel, Christian coffee mugs, even free Christian devotionals handed out at your church! Is this really what it's all about to claim Christ as your Savior and to love Him with all that you've got? I will answer with a simple word but you need to promise to finish today's reading so you get the full picture. The answer is "no." A Christian bubble approach to life is not and never was the plan. Now let's dive deeper so you get some context.

All of the things I mentioned at the start of today's reading are great things! I own many Christian hats, t-shirts and probably even a coffee mug or two. I have a friend who works for a Christian radio station. I am absolutely supportive of all these things. However, if they get in the way of an actual relationship with Christ then their intended target is being missed in a big way. The point of all these things is to spur on relationship with Him. They are meant to encourage us and help us, but they do not replace the action of opening His Word and getting the truth inside of us. And so if I had to choose between a t-shirt that says "It is Well" or each of us taking 20 minutes out of our day to read from Psalms, the choice is an easy one.

To love Christ above all else requires knowing Him. Growing in relationship with Him. Chasing after Him and His will for our lives. And this cannot be done with fun shirts and coffee mugs. Like any relationship, it will take time and effort. That is where our priorities should lie though: on the effort that it takes to be close with Christ. He desires nothing else and He deserves nothing less.

In its purest form, a Christian t-shirt is meant to serve as a reminder of our Savior. Maybe it looks cool; maybe the message is presented in a unique way, but the true desire is that it would simply point us back to Christ. Likewise, Christian radio and all the different artists who make worship music have just one goal: to help us draw nearer to Christ in our daily life.

Too often people are cynical about the desires of Christian musicians, like they are only out to make money or turn worship into entertainment. There are probably some unfortunate examples of that but for the most part, Christian worship leaders who put their music out there truly have just one goal: to encourage and inspire us to walk with Christ. (It is actually we who mess that up by idolizing the artists who are only trying to bring glory to the true Artist.)

So be on alert. Reduce the "noise" in your life and make sure that priority one is chasing Christ above all else. There are great tools that are presented to you and fun ways to keep Him at the center but the most basic and fundamental way to know Him is to read the Word, pray everyday and lift Him up in worship. All the rest is extra!

1) Have you placed anything ahead of investing in your relationship with Christ?

This is how God showed his love among us:
He sent his one and only Son into the world
that we might live through Him. **- 1 John 4:9**

Where do we think this idea of love came from, anyways? Christ isn't asking us to do anything that He didn't first do himself – and in the most amazing way possible. The love we give back to Him pales in comparison to the love He poured out on our behalf. He is the God who came to us, lived a perfect life and then poured out His blood on the cross as a sacrifice for all mankind. When He could have called scores of angels to save Him in the darkest moment humanity has ever known, He endured the cross anyways. He leaned in to the moment. He had faith that His Father would sustain Him through that trial and redeem all of us as a result.

It was not just His love for us that brought him through that moment; it was also His faith in the Father. We need to love Christ with total abandon, but we only can do that when we let faith power our love. Do we have faith in God that He will give us the strength to surrender our way of life and love Christ enough to embrace His plan for us? This is where the rubber truly meets the road.

We cannot attempt to love purely on our own strength, not our love for others or our love for Christ. The love we have been called to is honestly a supernatural love. It is a love we are incapable of possessing by ourselves. It requires a source that is not of this world – it requires faith in God the Father working through us!

The night that Christ was arrested and placed on trial, He prayed *"Father, if you are willing, take this cup from me; yet not my will but yours be done."* (Luke 22:42) He was surrendering His own will and trusting that the Father would sustain Him as He pursued the Father's will. This is the same prayer that we must pray. Our circumstances are certainly less intimidating, our outcome much more hopeful; but we need this same source for our love. We need a faith that is fueled by the Giver of faith. And if we will lean in, He will come through just as He did for Christ.

As we wrestle with the struggle of showing love to others who at times seem unlovable, we must remember who our source is. As we wrestle with the challenge of loving a Savior who has loved us in the deepest way any one ever could, we absolutely must remember who our source is! Without the assurance that our Father in heaven will supply us with the ability to love like this, it can be very intimidating. It is very intimidating. But through faith in Him it will be our reality!

1) Have you ever thought about the source of your love?

2) Have you believed by faith that God will give you the ability to love beyond your natural capabilities?

He asked them, "Who is it you want?"
And they answered, "Jesus of Nazareth."
Jesus answered, "I am he. If you are looking for me,
Then let these men go." - **John 18:7-8**

Faced with the most daunting outcome this world has ever known, Jesus Christ leaned in. When Judas arrived on the scene with a group of soldiers and religious leaders to take Jesus away, Christ stepped up to face the end that He did not deserve but was willing to endure. He did this for me and He did this for you. And it is one of a thousand reasons that He is our most beautiful Savior!

As Christ stepped into these final moments of His life on Earth, literally everything was on the line. This was what He had worked toward for 33 years as a human being and all 3 years of His active ministry. The fact that He embraced death on the cross is what validated all of His teachings and miracles. This proved His words to be true when He said *"Yet I am not alone, for my Father is with me"* in John 16:32. It was His relationship with the Father that gave him the strength and vision to do this. He knew the outcome and He knew it was worth it. He was on a mission to redeem His people from their sins – to reunite mankind with Father God. It was this crystal clear understanding of His role that empowered Him to come through when we needed Him most. It is simply beautiful.

I have done some ridiculously foolish things in my time on this earth. And so have you. Even if I haven't met you, I know it to be true. I've met enough people and talked through enough challenges to know that no one is exempt from stupidity. We all inflict it on others at times or endure it ourselves. But Jesus Christ made a way out. He did what only the Son of God could do and He bought our freedom. He paid the price so that we might know what it means to live completely free.

As we close this fourth and final week, I want to encourage you to really reflect on your Savior. Do you fully grasp what He did for you on that night? It is a beautiful choice of words that He used in this passage from John 18, *"if you are looking for me, then let these men go."*

I'm one of those men. He stepped in to my place and demanded my freedom as part of the deal. It is stunning. It is undeserved. And it exactly what the most beautiful Savior would do for His child. He did it for me, and He also did it for you.

Spend a few minutes praising Him for all that He has done in your life. And when you think you're about done, spend a few more minutes with Him. He more than deserves it!

1) Have you recognized the beauty and strength that Jesus Christ possessed on your behalf?

2) Have you spent time praising your Savior for His beautiful sacrifice?

Conclusion:

Taking This into Your Everyday Life

A final word from each author

We have come to the end and I now have the chance to say one final closing message. Easy enough, right? I mean, what else could need said? We have covered the spectrum pretty well if I do say so myself.

We encouraged you to break the chains of your past and step into the newness of life in Christ. We gave you practical ways to do that and Scriptures that show it is not only possible, but also God's plan for your life. We showed you how you can fight for hope by leaning on His truth and living it out in your day-to-day life.

We also talked about loving others well: what this looks like in real life and what God would have us do to make sure we are doing it how He intended. Lastly, we pointed out that without loving Christ above all, the rest is just hype. It is self-help from a Christian perspective. We must love Jesus deeply for any of this to truly work.

That brings us to these closing words. I have named this writing "All You've Got" because that's what it will take to walk this out in real life. But the thing is, this is not meant to be a discouragement. It is meant to be the greatest relief yet!

Obviously, I would not conclude a book on Hope with something discouraging. I want to take the pressure off and tell you the most exciting thing about this whole process: it works the best when you surrender. When you give up all that you have and welcome in all that Christ offers, the doors will blow open on your life. Your hopes will soar, your striving to perform will disappear, and He will have a willing heart to work in and through. That is what I mean by giving "all you've got." Stop holding on to what you think you have under control and embrace what He is offering.

For me, it is always about stewardship. If I had to preach one message 10 times in a row, it would be the message of stewardship. What are you doing with what you have been given? Are you trying to control it? Are you trying to force something you want instead of what God is trying to offer in your life? Or are you doing the best you can with what you have where you are – even if it's not your favorite thing. You do know that God has only your best in mind, right? Lean in to the gifts He has given you and steward them well. It will completely transform your life! Give all you've got to what He's gifted you in and do it as an act of worship. That's an offering He will always bless!

So often we adopt the ways of the world into our Christianity. We attempt to run at things like the world does and hope it will bring fruit in our Christian life. But we know how we get fruit – through abiding in Him. The answer isn't hidden; it is in plain sight. So my encouragement to you would be this: abide in Him, trust in His plan for your life and give 100% to what He has entrusted you with today, then leave the results to God. He keeps score. He has a plan. He has a will for your life. The role you play is one of surrender followed by obedience. It's the most hope-filled way to live that I have known in my 32 years on this earth. When I work for my plans, I can easily lose heart. When I run towards His, I am never discouraged. Lean in, friends! Give him all you've got and let Him give back all that He has planned. That will certainly get your hopes up!

-QCL

It is our prayer at this point in the study, you are sensing and understanding that there is hope. There is hope in every situation that you face. There is hope even on your darkest days. There is always hope if you will search it out. But it is pivotal to know where to look to find it.

Our hope is not in the government.
Our hope is not in our beauty or outward appearance.
Our hope does not lie in our IQ or GPA.
Our hope is not in our accomplishments or our resume.
Our hope is in Christ. Our hope alone, forever and always, lies in the sweet, saving grace of Jesus Christ. Apart from Christ, there is no hope!

We are praying this over you and every other reader who finds this book. We hope you pray with us:

I pray that the eyes of your heart may be enlightened in order that you may know the HOPE to which he has called you, the riches of his glorious inheritance in his holy people, and his incomparably great power for us who believe. That power is the same as the mighty strength he exerted when he raised Christ from the dead and seated him at his right hand in the heavenly realms.
- Ephesians 1:18-20

In Christ we have hope!

-NS

Notes_____

_____

_____

_____

_____

_____

_____

_____

_____

_____

_____

_____

_____

_____

_____

_____

_____

_____

_____

_____

_____